GROTESQUE WEATHER AND GOOD PEOPLE

괴괴한 날씨와 착한 사람들

Grotesque Weather and Good People

by Lim Solah

Translated by Oh Eunkyung and Olan Munson

Black Ocean
Boston - Chicago

To reprint, reproduce, or transmit electronically, or by recording all or part of this manuscript, beyond brief reviews or educational purposes, please send a written request to the publisher at:

Black Ocean
P.O. Box 52030
Boston, MA 02205
blackocean.org

Cover Art and Design by Abby Haddican | abbyhaddican.com
Book Design by Taylor D. Waring | taylordwaring.com

ISBN: 978-1-939568-43-4
Library of Congress Control Number: 2021953196

This book was published with the support of a publication and translation grant from the Daesan Foundation.

FIRST EDITION

CONTENTS

PART 3

PART 4

TRANSLATORS' NOTE

In some ways, we played the expected roles of native informant to each other as co-translators: Eunkyung presuming authority in her native Korean and Olan in her native English; but then again, the collaborative process is not nearly so simple, nor is our relationship to these languages. We take our cues from Lim Solah's poems, full of "me's" that watch each other, overlap, multiply, disappear, and reappear.

The Korean 나(na) can present the self as either subject or object, depending on the particle attached to it. The subject particles -는(neun) and -가(ga) would transform the 나 into an "I", and the object particle -를(leul) would translate 나 into "me" or "myself."

In the Korean of Lim Solah's poems, there is an added strangeness. Even when the self is grammatically marked as a subject, there is something object-like about it ("Today there were plenty of me's"). At other times, the self is overtly made to be the object ("With all the other models, I set myself down.")

This is why, when the translation might have first called for "I," we favored the slightly stranger, slightly tenser option "me" or "myself;" and when a reflexive pronoun such as "myself" or "ourselves" would've been more grammatically correct, we opted for the agrammatical "me" or "we." In so doing, we hoped to draw attention to the way the 나 of Lim Solah's poems flickers in and out of subjecthood and objecthood. In a collaborative translation, the apparent unidirectionality of translating from Korean into English also gets muddled. Questions are raised: who made the final call? Who wrote the first draft? Who translated, who interpreted, who edited, and who stylized? As Lim Solah might say, "at different times a different person" did.

We are grateful to the many other members of our translators' "we"— our editors at Black Ocean, Jake Levine, and Carrie Olivia Adams. A generous grant from the Daesan Foundation. Lim Solah, for these poems and for her kind correspondence. *Puerto del Sol*, *The Margins*, *Salt Hill*, *Poetry Daily*, and *Lana Turner*, for being the first platforms through which Lim's poems appeared in English. And our friends, colleagues, and instructors at the Literature Translation Institute of Korea, from whom we learned translation.

PART I

POMEGRANATE

The window shows me: me standing outside the window. A road crosses over my thighs, and the last train arrives into my waist. People pour out and walk into a building inside my chest. I put my hand in my chest and open a window. There's a woman inside repotting her plant. I open another window below the first one. There's a split pomegranate on the kitchen table. I open another window below the one I just opened. There's white. A small baby grabs fistfuls of snow and crawls over a snow-covered field. I open the next window down. The street lamps light up on my eyebrows. An airplane passes over my forehead. The city in my body oozes out. I open the last window. I see me standing inside, counting windows. The glass glitters. I turn off the light. Me inside the window, me outside the window. We can finally disappear.

SAND

Today there were plenty of me's.
I read all the junk mail until none was left.

I watched water drops hang desperately from the handrail
until they were gone.
I cheered for them to fall.

I counted the leaves on my ivy
for the first time. Numbers jumbled with the ivy vine.
I felt fooled.

Seekers wonder where hiders are
and hiders wonder where seekers are. But me,
I wonder about wonder.

Like scribbles on a cast,
pain is popular with sentences.

Today I draw the national flag of a nation that doesn't exist.
Proud that only I can draw it

I take off my socks and put them on a naked plush pig.
Compared to the pig, I'm short two legs.

When I stare at the red blinking dot at the top of a building
I blink.
I forgot how to forget I'm blinking.
I'm at a loss for what to do.

Today there's no end to the me's.
I heap me's up like a mound of sand
and try to count them until none are left.

"I'm not alone," you say, but I wonder
how long you were.

BEAUTIFUL

I hang the ocean
in a frame.

I've seen myself sinking into the ocean.
My limbs corroded
into coral.

The ashen limbs
were stuck between coral.
Yellow or blue fish loitered about.

Look, there's a tropical fish, said some scuba divers
pointing toward me. They tore wet bread and threw it.
Leaving the word "beautiful" in the coral forest
the divers headed back to land.

Leaving myself behind, I also
exited my dream.

People who have left this place said
the earth is a beautiful planet, but
because here is the only place I've ever
lived, I want to prove that here is hell.

Leaving myself here, again I exit
and slip

between the butcher shop and dry cleaners.
I stand and look at a sign that says "For Lease."
In an empty store, Mother Mary sits alone
sewing a quilt.

Again, on the ocean
I hang this frame.

LINT

I'm touching my empty pocket
with my empty hand.

Something inside?
Something inside.

Inside the pocket
is another pocket, bright and square,
falling on the floor.

A messy, furry dog
slowly sneaks into the pocket and
rests there in silence.

As the pocket shifts
the dog moves with it, and

into a different empty pocket
another dog is on its way.
As coal-black clouds gather, the bright pocket disappears.

Above the clouds an invisible dog is sitting.
It is strangely bright.
The dog is quiet, resting up there.

The weather outside the weather.
I wonder about the real weather at the end of it.
The tips of my toes dispose of temperature.
Wanting to have a pocket again, I wait.

There's nothing in your pocket, right?
I turn the pocket inside out.
Lint.

Since the dog I thought would come did not
I dig around the seam of the pocket and
scrape out the lint.

FORECAST

I feel like I'm a weather forecaster.
When spring comes, I say here comes spring.
When it's raining, I say it's raining.
Here and there the weather is generally the same and generally
    different. So I tell people about the weather.
The weather keeps moving somewhere even as I'm telling someone
    about the weather.
Even as the weather report arrives, new weather arrives at me.
How many weathers live here?
With a blazingly sunny school ground, with a thickly-wooded dark
    cedar forest,
with a reservoir freezing around the edges, with an old man leaning
    against an empty stroller he walks.
I often hear that I seem like a good person.
It's generally the same and generally different from hearing that I'm an
    evil person.
My goodwill repeats the same word. It speaks over and over again like
    a forecast bound to the future tense.
My goodwill looking dapper, willingly worries and willingly warns me.
Bearing a smile, it confines me.
I open the window. I push out the grotesque weather and good people
    that have stagnated inside.
What nice weather today.

BENCH

I said goodbye to two different people by this bench.
At different times a different person sat here and waited for me.
Whenever I walk by the bench one or the other is seated here.
Sunlight passes through the top of one person's head. Nothing shades him.
Raindrops pass through the other's lap. *Okay, let's quit it.*

I touch the rain that passed through people.
The one who isn't here is at my fingertips.

A white, dried leaf hangs from a branch.
A different dried white leaf
disappears into the distance. The leaves fall, dead—they're innumerous.

Every day I paint over one person,
and every day I experience one person fading away.

Yes, let's quit saying, "Let's quit it."

Our seats are gone.
The chair that's long been empty must be reserved and
I'm not sorry, so the sorriness lingers.

BASICS

I walk around looking for a white t-shirt
for tomorrow's plans.

I enter a clothing store. White t-shirts are gathered
close to each other. They have or don't have chest pockets.

I enter the next store. White t-shirts are piled up
with other t-shirts, crumpling one another.
Crumpled shirts are less expensive.

Faceless
mannequins look good in anything. I walk around
to find a t-shirt that looks good with my face.
It's basic to have basic t-shirts, a salesperson

says. While walking around to find a white t-shirt, I remember
the white t-shirts I have at home. Since I basically have them
I head back

and open my drawers.
I take out all the items that are white.
Every white t-shirt has its own stain.

I squat down and apply toothpaste to the stains
then scrub. I gaze at the disappearing stains
as if they're fading Polaroids, the faces turning white.

Removable stains
are removed, unremovable stains
are unremoved. The clothes that look best on me are
the most stained because I wear them the most often.

I take out the spin-dried t-shirts from the washing machine and
give them a hard shake. I hang them by the window. The t-shirts
are flapping. As they dry, they grow much brighter.
The bright smell of the faceless laundry
fills my room.
Tomorrow I have plans.

TOAD AND ME

I like how stones stare at me.
At night, I sit on a bench in a field of pebbles.

Their eyes sparkle and
so do mine.

I don't move.
A shadow over there
doesn't move either.

I hurl a stone at the shadow.
I like that the shadow doesn't budge.
I throw a bigger stone.

We are Gemini.
Twins talking into paper cups on a string phone.

Two three-hundred-year-old ginkgo trees
lap up muddy water together.

Two starved roe deer come down to the village.
The sound of gunfire rises like firecrackers.
Echoes of gunfire are served

and the deer share it like warm soup.
The shadow of a cloud with a pockmarked face
lays down its head.

Everyone shares the pattern on the toad
like scarlet fever.

I like that me is multiplying.
I grow bigger after all.

FOX

A dog stands on the ball.
A clown holds the flute.
I wind up the spring.

Inside the glass
the dog and the clown turn in circles.
To the dog, it must look like the woods are turning.

I rotate the spring
and the woods transform into a music box. Inside the woods are me,
my basketball, a water bottle,
and a fox.

I look in the music box inside the music box.
The music plays without the clown blowing the flute.
The moon slips through every tree
even though I don't throw the ball.

Though they do nothing but circle,
the spring winds down. The air slips out
from the basketball.
I twist the cap of the water bottle.
A mountain crowned with perpetual snow shines onto the bottle.
There's still water inside.

A Turkish boy practices the Sufi
in his white dress.
He whirls and whirls in place until he
loses balance.
He says this opens a way to talk with God.

I stick a needle in the basketball
and fill it with air.
The air makes the ball firm.
I kick it hard.

The trees spew rain
when the rain stops and the wind blows.

Rain is only visible in the headlights.
Into the headlights
a fox jumps.

MAY

A dandelion puff floats through the air. I catch it. A white spider bursts inside my palm. I walk with my hand balled in a fist. Shadows redefine the forest's eyes, ears, nose, mouth. The hair of the forest lengthens. The bark is cracked. Birds nest on the crowns of the trees, and I reach up to touch my hair whorl.

A footprint made by a bare foot plunged into a puddle. The bare feet of May built a park. Bunches of flowers bloomed, and bunches of flowers fell. I sit on a cold rock and stagnate.

Dark fragments never return. Dark fragments are leaves dragged along the ground. I pick up a leaf I stepped on and dust it off. I'm certain that these grew from my flesh. My fingers get wet. The leaf leaks water from its dark veins. We exchange cuts. Bone to bone, the leaf and I touch.

Stag beetle grubs develop into their homes. The flowers of May are spewed into existence. All together, they grin. May flowers are perfect. In May they die.

ZOO

Black mayflies hover around black eyes. I pick a dead mayfly out
from those eyes with my fingertips.
There are polar bears at the zoo

even in hot countries.
The bear sprawled out

on a melting block of ice
doesn't know what a polar bear or the North Pole is.
But even the bear knows
that this is not the North Pole.
My mouth agape

I sit on a subway loop in the mornings.

It rains and
raindrops gather at the tips of my rolled umbrella.
The drops trickle down my body.

They gather into a puddle underneath my soles.
Drop
Drop
Drop

A lake remains. The train crosses the North Pole. I get off
the subway loop. I leave that puddle behind me.

SPARE

Shrrip—I heard a ripping sound.
As my head fell off
rolled to the ground and disappeared

I was thinking, *I'm
dead*, but now I wonder

how many lives
have I left to spare?
Cupping my cold knees with both hands
the knees melt down.
The knees fade away.

Although I'm disappearing
I feel like I'm coming to life.

I've never met the things
that keep me alive.

How does my heart look?
Is it pretty and red?

Snowflakes bloom on my knees.
I open my coat and tuck my knees into it.

On a spare button attached inside the coat
I see a face that looks like mine.

I'm thinking, it's
black and round, but

THE SAME

Sand colored crabs on the sand. They watch the sea all day,
hear footsteps in the distance
and dig a hole to scurry to.

Styrofoam boats drift away. Even though the net is loose like a spider's
web, fish get trapped. The rainy season flops and flails between dry
seasons.

There comes a time when even water drops abandon their clouds.
There is a time when boys, stripped down to their pants, are like sand
colored crabs. Hiding in their unlit houses. Their dark doorways gasp
like tiny holes in the sand.

There is no way besides this:
An old man, damp in the rain,
carefully threads a fishing line through the hook.
Silvery sardines thread their mouths quick with rusted hooks.

Extreme hardship also arrives at the country under the sea.
Each footstep that chases this country is a life threat.
Fish sharpen their bones to survive.

Barefooted boys climb tall trees again. Branch by branch, they get
farther from their shoes. Climbing and climbing. They get higher
and higher. Under the same weather, low and high appear at the same
time.

The holes deepen like cliffs.
Gushing from a single hole
thousands of ants.

HANDSHAKE

I sit in a park and try what stones do. I draw in my arms and legs and hug them tight. I won't let my insides get wet even if it rains. Let's call this a welcome. A sparrow flies over and pecks at a stone. It puckers its mouth like an arrow and gives the stone a kiss. Let's consider this a handshake. Let's say we meet a stone with lots of holes. In each hole a greeting that we could pluck out and read.

The wind blows. A shuttlecock that rolls alone rolls by itself. It becomes a stone that remembers birds.

Another wind, a sandstorm. Tiny bits of stone peck my eyes. Disheveled like windblown hair, I follow the wind. The birds' beaks cheer for the stones to break. The grit of sand in my mouth. Crunch. Let's call this a promise. My body holes fill with sand.

MYSELF

Through my shadow, me can watch me. The place where our shadows overlap like a net becomes our home. No matter who steps on it, or however many steps it takes, our home grows secure. It slowly moves around the floor.

A cloud's shadow blows into the room, and a breeze stirs somewhere far beyond the window. The cloud's shadow starts at my toes and passes through me. A winged insect flies in and out of the cloud's shadow. Bit by bit, faraway things cover me from head to foot.

Me stays here for a long time.
Shadows are more like life than life.
Me hands my shadow to anyone and anything.
Me lives overlapped with everyone.
No one has ever touched me.

THE JUNGGYE RIVER

The benches are wet. There's no choice. I've got to walk.

Carp swim in the Junggye River near Wangsimni Station. A rat
paddles after them. Its head moves up and down. Down and up.

Look at that rat. Some might be carp, some pathetic rats. People, the more I
follow you, the more I become a lie.

I gasp like the rat's head poking out from the water.
I exclude myself over and over. Whatever shakes is like a hand gesture.

On a billboard screen, Cirque du Soleil.
From inside a person's suit another person walks out.
One after another, more people walk out. In twos and threes, they
breathe fire like conversation.

I want to be a circus member and perform impossibilities.
I want to be round-eyed with wonder like I'm watching the circus for the first
time. I want to swim against my breath like a rat chasing carp.

Dead bodies float only after they sink.
I'm wet with the benches. At last I walk.

PART 2

9 YEARS OLD

I often played
a city building game. Planted trees,
made lakes,
erected buildings

and expanded roads. The citizens were
honest and diligent. When I got bored

I would drop a child
into a lake. *Help!*

I watched
how long the screaming child
would last. From time to time

I'd let the survivors go on living.
Or throw them back in the water. No matter
how many I killed, the city remained quiet.
I set buildings

on fire.
I created hurricanes, spread disease and called UFOs to ravage the
clean, tidy roads. My kind-hearted people shrieked and ran around.

Their hair aflame. They fled my city. So I enclosed it
with a wall. But I didn't

burn all.
I destroyed the city
just enough for my people to restore it.
To keep the fun going.
To play the game longer.

I'm sorry, my people. I don't
feel sorry. I just don't.

A few accidents and misfortune
is how my citizens get diligent.

TRANSFER

While people with flawless central angles roll by, relaxed like long
sleek spokes, the cripple grinds his leg against the ground like grinding
teeth. His kneecaps grow larger than his knees.

A crippled planet with a half ring limps forever throughout the
universe. Its imperfect orbit invades the perfect orbit of another
planet.

Thousands of shooting stars fall like holly olives.
Small animals stand in awe as if God is shedding tears.
Out of all of us, only the crippled intervene in the universe.

A cripple walks. Starting with the closest bodies with magnetism,
the cripple pulls, performing the law of gravitation in his own body,
transforming guardrails into body parts, closing the distance between
himself and people walking behind, moving his body from line 1 to
line 2, from a cold handle to an even colder passenger.

A dog with a triple time gait crosses over to Earth like a parallel
universe. One universe carrying two universes on its back follows.

You cripple as you peep into the rifts in the air. With one foot resting
on a stair, you creak like a ballerina on a music box with broken gears.

PLATFORM

Are you alright? The child replies that she lost her way home in search
of her lost red shoe(god).
She tries to hold up falling memories
like oversized pants.

Whenever the shoe(god) lost me I found myself at the last station, at
the mulberry tree. I'd pick up the mulberries and leave my teeth marks
on something mulberry red.

The child walks the platform
with bare, red feet.
I take the child to the lost-and-found. There are only lost keys and
bags, but no shoe(god).

I must find my shoe(god).
Passengers step out and the subway lights turn off. The child boards
the train. Carrying the red child, the dark train sets off on a route that
no one has ever travelled.

The shoe(god), too, searches for people in this way. Which is probably
how it lost its way home.
Was it waiting to be asked, *Are you alright?*
Things in the lost-and-found were never meant to be abandoned.
Just misplaced.

T V

Is it really that sad? In celebration of the 70th Independence Day,
there's a TV special that features Namdaemun on fire.

He rubs his nose in his hand, as if applying lotion.

So heartbreaking. That's our first national treasure! He sobs.

I tear up as I watch a kid's science show. They cut a hole in the cow's
belly and

the kids insert their hands. Dear cow. You blink your big round eyes.

The kids take a pile of mucus-covered cud out of your belly. You lick it,
dripping drool.

I blow my nose, wipe my tears, and watch TV.

Kathmandu collapses. Breaking news.

800 killed. No. 4000. The dead increase as I write this poem.

Why don't you cry? He doesn't cry because it's not his country.

I gather all the TV tragedy and broadcast this poem.

I watched a documentary about a dictator who massacred to fulfill his dream of making the human race superior.

And saw the story of the dead woman who was dragged downtown by her hair.

Hundreds of people just stood by and watched. I munch on chips as I write this down.

Cries escape from under the rubble. "What's your name? Answer me! The rescue team is on its way!"

If you want to live, say something! I say to the TV.

The TV dozes off, and I wake it up.

I enter the TV. There he stands, behind the bus barricade.

We face each other. This means confrontation.

Across the barricade, I wish he would turn around.

I let myself turn. Only when you turn your back can you watch the same TV.

MODEL

I want to see a giraffe.
I go to see a giraffe.

I fail to see a giraffe
so I make a giraffe.

I place the giraffe next to the earth. Next to the earth
is a hero, smiling, with his face turning one hundred and eighty degrees.

I want to see the earth
so I spin the earth.

There are more oceans than Earths.
Why is it called Earth and not Ocean?

There is no giraffe in the giraffe
no earth in the Earth
and no human in humans.
That's why I like them.

When you fail to see what you want to, you make a fake.
I become a model that looks human.

This world is just a model of some other world.
Our hands that built this world

tear it apart
because we don't see the world we wanted.

A world walks out of the world. But it's no use.
With all the other models, I set myself down.

TO BE CONTINUED

"And the troika flew forward, 'devouring space,' and the closer he came to his goal, the more powerfully the thought of her again, of her alone, took his breath away and drove all the other terrible phantoms from his heart."*

Dmitri wears a bloodied coat. The carriage races on, carrying candy, toffee, and pistols. The old man has been struck down. Dmitri makes haste for his beloved. His cart loaded with champagne that he bought with some other woman's money.

Racing carriage scenes have always fascinated me. No matter what, they create a climax. When you're trying to get away from something most horrible, or when you set off to save something most precious, it's always the carriage that's on the move. You wield your whip and race on. How beautiful to see those horses run like hell while thrashed. And the carriage that speeds up as their pain mounts. The coachman who strikes harder as his fear grows. He is the one who lashes at the horses but shudders as if beaten. *"Father, do you not see the Erlking?"***

I love the Erlking.*** I love how the father rides with his son in arm. How the Erlking keeps appearing in a wisp of fog or in the old branches of willow trees. When the Erlking whispers to the son to come with him, the father rides as fast as the burning fuses of dynamite sticks. The harder he avoids destruction, the closer he approaches. The faster he runs from the Erlking, the closer he approaches. The further he escapes from death, the closer it approaches. How delightful.

45

"You kilt my maw!"
I strike again and again
and *"run in the dust."*
I cry, looking at the stick.
*"Mother was a horse."*****

When there's nothing left to do but run, the carriage hits the road. Your life at stake in that carriage. The sentences rush like a racing carriage, the horses and words that I abused rampage. The night is sucked into the black water. A strong current tips the carriage. The wheels are swept off. Your body shakes; the night crosses over, in one big stride—

*"Iona sits on the box without stirring, bent as double as the living body can be bent."****** I open the window, stick out my head, and dry the cold sweat off my brow. The wildness of the wind persists.

——

"There was one moment when he felt an impulse to stop Andrey, to jump out of the cart, to pull out his loaded pistol, and to make an end of everything without waiting for the dawn" (Dostoevsky's "Brothers Karamazov," Chapter VI, translation by Constance Garnett)

**"Will you, sweet lad, come along with me?
My daughters shall care for you tenderly;
In the night my daughters their revelry keep,*

They'll rock you and dance you and sing you to sleep."
(Schubert/Goethe's "Erlkönig," translation by Edwin Zeydel)

*** I'm bad at singing. I don't really want to be a good singer but there is a song that I want to sing well. I listen to "the Erlking." It requires four different voices: the Narrator, the Father, the Son and the Erlking. I narrate myself. I hold myself in the arm and run. I, in my own arms, shudder in fear. I lure myself and chase. I am swallowed up by myself and dead in my arms. I open my mouth wide and keep singing "The Erlking."

*****"Your mother was a horse, but who was your father, Jewel?"* (Faulkner, "As I Lay Dying")

******"Just as the young man had been thirsty for water, he thirsts for speech. His son will soon have been dead a week, and he has not really talked to anybody yet . . . He want talk of it properly, with deliberation . . . He wants to tell how his son was taken ill, how heffered, what he said before he died, how he died."* (Anton Chekhov's "Misery," translation by Constance Garnett)

PART 3

LIKE DOGS

White-eyed Dog,
please take the milk from my school lunch.
I'm sick of drinking white milk.

The dog stares

with pupils blank-white
like milk.
It stares at the black-eyed child.

The dog's white eyes
are inside the child's black pupils.

The dog's white eyes
are inside the dog's white pupils.

The child spills some milk and walks away.
The alley quickly narrows
to fit itself into the child's round pupils.
The dog trails behind

the child: a new path. But because the dog
is at her heels
the child is lost.

She throws a rock at the dog
and finds her way back.

The dog barks and
a chorus of dogs bark
behind all the front gates
of the houses.

The child passes.
She vanishes behind a dark cement wall.

Utility poles twist
themselves into the child's pupils.

Get lost, White-eyed Dog.
I'm not your food.

This afternoon
void with hunger
people crouch like dogs
at the front gate
of a house they don't own.

RENT

I stand and gaze out the empty store's window.
I watch people pass. They walk with profiles directed straight ahead.

Little kids go by in the afternoon.
In the afternoon's second phase
students walk past in school uniforms.
A lady with a backpack slung over her chest
sticks a flyer for a Chinese restaurant on the door.
My reflection emerges on the window in the afternoon's third phase.
Car headlights come and go.

I put bread dough in a plastic bag and the dough slowly rises. The bag
rises too. I hold my nose to the bag and inhale just as slowly. The scent
bursts outside when I open the door.

A man walking straight turns his head.
We meet eyes. He comes in, fumbling with his bag.

"I'll take one of these please."
I grab a roll with a pair of tongs because
my hands that made this bread are no longer allowed to touch it.

5,000 won an hour.
5,500 won per bread roll.
I wish I could eat the bread I make.

The man leans his black umbrella against the counter
and accepts the bread.
The back of his head dims.
He disappears with the roll.

A black umbrella left behind.
We stand in this empty store.
The umbrella and me.

I SCRATCH MY RIBS

I get bed bugs. Watching a couple of crows affably tear apart a rat.
As I sit and do nothing in particular on a street where nothing in
particular is happening. As I wet my hands in the sacred river. In some
part of the landscape, somewhere you'll never know.

I get bed bugs. Because bed bugs can't be seen, can't be heard, they
don't get sick, just bite and bite. Because the harder you work to get
rid of bed bugs, the worse they bite. I scratch my ribs when no one's
looking. I become a giant bed bug where other bed bugs live.

I dread my own body, like a watermelon tumbling down a steep slope.
Rolling scares me. Stopping scares me.

There are grains of sand that know this: the landscape looks still but
it's actually crumbling apart with all its strength. Like a bird suspended
midair. The bird flew for its life.

It's the bed bugs, not me, that bite me to live. It's not me but the bed
bugs who discover my body. The bed bugs get it right.
What a sight.

KEVIN CARTER

Collapsed. The keeled over moped spinning its tires.
Passengers poke their necks out the bus window. Busses avoid the
wreck. Parents cover their children's eyes and quietly pass.
I feel around for a severed ankle.

Collapsed. I clutch fistfuls of soil. I squeeze long, writhing coils with
my fingers and rub them back into the ground.
Yuck. Not for eating. I brush off my palms and stand up.
Pieces of worms crawl off in different directions.

Collapsed. I pick a cigarette butt off the ground,
clench it with my teeth.
He offers a lighter. *Are you alone? Do you have somewhere to stay tonight?*
I'm only trying to help. He sits next to me. A hand travels up my knee.

Collapsed. I pull up the withered milkvetch.
Plant a sunflower in its place.
Good work. Looks prettier already. The teacher examines the garden.
The classroom chairs we left outside absorb the rain. They warp over
time.

We have to stop doing such terrible things. It's despicable
a Lebanese person tells me.
I agree
I reply. A plate in my hands.
The veal on the grill smells delicious.

Our eyes meet. On that highway. A few more steps. You drag yourself.
You start to collapse as you stare at the trail of intestines.
I turn, no need to keep looking. I already got my shot.

DID YOU FEEL THE URGE TO KILL?

It's the kind of weather that smells like baby powder
so I prop open the door. *Pitter patter.* Something trickles inside.
Our eyes lock.

"Sir, there's a mouse in here."
"You left the door open. Call pest control."

I look for the mouse myself. I pick up beer bottles. I check under
boxes and a bag of flour. The mouse darts out from between the beer
bottles and behind the bag of flour. It risks its life in one swift gesture.
I do not.
Little dark holes huddle like mice. I grab a shovel from storage. The
last time I held a shovel like this was when I buried that dead pigeon. I
cut my breath off. *As soon as I see it, I'll beat that mouse to death.*

"Did you feel the urge to kill?" The reporter interrogates. The twelve-
year-old Filipino murderer scratches his scalp and shakes his head.
"My siblings were starving, and all I had to do was pull a trigger."
"Don't you feel bad? The victim had a family too."
"If I didn't take the money, someone else would've."

"Are you open?"
A woman enters. A scarf wound around her neck. I nod.
"Come in! I'm just reorganizing."
A mouse transforms the store. I wipe off sweat with my palm.

HOW?

The flower print dress I forgot about
gets caught on my fingers.
How strange. That I used to wear something like this.
I pull out more strange clothes and try them on.

When I grab a kitchen knife to kill myself
I find a rice paddle in my hand.
I shovel rice into my mouth with the paddle. And just like that,

"Have you eaten?" asks my mom.
I hang up.
Why do we always have to talk about rice?
These days I eat everything.

Black soybeans, cotton swabs, drain cleaner, Saejol Station on the 8th at 3pm.
Pay rent. 330,000 won.

I jotted this on a Post-it so I wouldn't forget.
But I forget where I put it.

Black soybeans in the refrigerator. Utterly, blackly, forgotten.
Why do small sprouts grow on these rancid beans?

Mom spreads her toast with moldy jam.
"It's still sweet."

Mom gulps expired milk.
"It tastes just fine."
Whenever the words *I want to die* boil inside me.

I scoop rice in my mouth
just like Mom.

Mom must've held the rice paddle in her hand too.
She must've reached for the rice paddle first thing in the morning.

How come I can't forget the taste of rice?
How do the necks of flowers twist
together towards the sun?
How is wonder so gross?

Again I clasp the broken watch on my wrist
and put on the flower print dress.
I flop down into a flower garden
flowerless.

WHITE

When I turn off the lights
someone reads the thoughts
I had in the light.

The stories I met
in the daytime touched the sun
and burned.

The rabbit on the veranda
had big ears, white fur.
It grew plump by the day.

While I was gone
in the daytime, the rabbit gnawed the wallpaper
and nibbled the desk and licked my sneakers.
Then one day it died.

I suck blood oozing from my
chewed-up lips.
Why did you do it?
I don't remember
a murderer says.
I change the channel
to a different death.

In the unlit room
I sit. Someone groans
like a person that's sick.

The rabbit died
the day I gave it a bath. I wash someone's black shadow
with my two hands.
I remember things I couldn't remember back then
.replies the murderer.

I turn on the lights
and continue the thoughts
of someone in the dark.

White fog
wrapped around the building
when I step outside.

EXPRESS

People I don't know enter my home.
A woman takes my rice bowls. A man drags my bike away. People make off with my dresser. Unfamiliar walls appear. My house becomes a house I don't know.

Even in a maze, I wouldn't lose my way
as long as my hand is on the wall.
I peer into the wall
and my hand lands on a pattern I've never seen before.

There used to be a vase here.
The flowers were pretty
even when they only had stems.
One time I filled the vase with water and drank.
Another time I kept my body under the blanket and stretched out just my neck.

A man drops the vase. It shatters.
A woman puts my music box in the dresser.
She sets my brush on the bookshelf. The people I don't know leave, and a wall I don't know surrounds me. Now the house is complete. I wipe away the footprints and drape a coat over a chair. Me and my clothes, we sit face to face.

MY FIRST RICE COOKER

I got a rice cooker that makes the rice just right.
I put it where my first rice cooker used to go.

It has the nerve to speak.
"Starting to cook"
"Your rice is ready."

The rice is like the first snow. Free of footprints. I stuff a spoonful into my mouth as soon as it's done. With the other hand I pick up stray grains and return them to my mouth. I erase myself blank.

I toss my old rice cooker next to the other stuff. All perfectly usable. I turn my back. My red rice cooker. I salvaged it from the electronics repair shop. It was the smallest one, but still a bit too big for just me. It had a single button, and I used it to boil rice, make porridge, bake bread, and steam potatoes. It choo-choo'd like a train, traveling the unknown past through yesterday to today. I always arrive at the platform too early. I wait and wait for the rice to cook.

I once saw a street vendor present an offering of rice. The vendor wrapped a flower and a handful of rice with a banana leaf and set it at the foot of the gate. Burned incense and prayed. Night teetered, then collapsed. A dog slowly approached. It ate the offering. It lapped up the black masses of ants swarming the rice, careful not to miss a single grain. Watching the scene, I hated these prayers for food and wealth a little less.

Abundant snowfall.
Snowflakes white as rice.

Next to my red rice cooker
an abandoned red kettle.

BRUISE

Filthy.
With water I wash the scum stuck to the water bottle.

How does invisible air touch a banana? Does the air bruise it? A bruising
banana is tastier.
Rainwater washed the window yesterday. On today's window it left a
transparent stain.

At some point young me started stalking me. *Piss off, idiot,* I said, and
the child cried like mush. She crumpled her bruised face in front of me
like she wanted me to see.
There is, at times, a crumpled child in front of me.
I show young me to people on days I want to be loved.
They offer me hugs.

I take a crumpled newspaper and just manage to erase the window
stain. I look outside and
eat a bruised banana.

INSTEAD OF

I once stretched out my arms to hold the body smell
that lingered in an empty room.
As always, the body smells were bigger than their people.

I look at the photo.
In the memory
of me crying
I'm smiling.

A child tries to suck a big toe instead of its thumb.
Walks on hands and knees instead of feet.
Instead of a mobile
its shadow
revolves on the wall.

WHILE

I go to drink the vending machine lights. I insert the coins I was fiddling with. I like how the machine lights up. I like shaking hands with paper cups. Warm as newborn quails. I like engraving teeth marks on the rim. I leave the cup on a chair. It becomes trash, becomes a letter.

I like how raindrops call out to me tenaciously on stormy nights. I like how they call my name twice. My name that is hard to pronounce. I cast off clothes to pretend I don't know my own name. I like pulling those clothes over my head. I like my body thawing in the downpour. Assailed by that downpour. I like how demons and angels below the Catholic steeple corrode in equal measure.

Raindrops will collect in the paper cup note. The drops will gather and engrave a cloud. The abundant spring-green hands of a sycamore will flutter. This is how it gestures both farewell and fare well. This is how I leave while I stay.

BEHIND

Footstep sounds close in. Close in tight.

The silence of the roadside trees grows pointed. Shadows sharpen.

At the corner, I whirl around.
"Who goes there? Why are you following me?" *I was worried about you walking alone at night.* You stare at me. My secrets, unknown to me, pile around my feet. Unknown to me, the secrets are swift growing branches. They impersonate me.

We sit for a while in a park and observe the slide. The bright side of the slide is empty. The dark side hides.

There is no one. And yet the sensor light flickers. On. Off. A cat appears. Vanishes.

THE BAG

A woman peers into
the bag in her arms.

A lunch cart whizzes by. Then a tunnel.
Her long hair dangles
as she looks in the bag.

We cross the bridge and
the bag wriggles. It lets out a small cry.
The woman glances around.
Passengers stare.

She inserts her hand.
The bag quiets down.

In my bag
I see blue water under black water. Clear water
under blue water. A white coral reef beneath the clear water.
Silver fish between the white coral.

I sprinkled salt in the fishbowl when my fish got sick.
For a while it helped.
Then the fish swallowed a lump of salt
and died anyway.

Mom made her way to Dad's office
with a kitchen knife in her bag.
She clutched it to her chest
and gripped my hand.

I send her a text
that I had dinner with Dad.
Sushi at a new Japanese place.
She says she's making the pickled chili peppers
that Dad likes so much.

TRAGEDY

A fallen persimmon under a persimmon tree. No one bothers to pick it up. Alone, it sits there and works hard to get mushy. It blackens inch by inch. The world has turned a blind eye to this rotting persimmon.

My grandma never ate rice cakes. They were too hard to chew. She scarfed down beef steak happily despite having no teeth. I chewed hard on the rice cakes left on the plate.

Dad gave me a one thousand *won* bill to buy my grandma chrysanthemum cakes. Those browned chrysanthemum-shaped cakes. Once fresh, now flabby inside the paper bag. I ate them all in front of Grandma's bedroom door.

"When someone dies there is no such thing as a happy end. All death is sad," my sister wept. *Well, a happy end is a happy end. It is what it is.* I swallow slices of boiled pork. The tragedy was flimsy.

"When I'm old, I'll shower all the time." "What do you mean, Mom?" "You hate the smell of old people. You won't go near them." "I don't hate how old people smell. I've just never known an old person who loved me."

I return with a paper bag filled with chrysanthemum cakes and go into Grandma's room. I sit on the cushion she always sat on, cover myself in the blanket she always used, and I eat the cakes. The more I try to remember it, the more the smell fades.

THAT'S WHY

Apricot blossoms are terrifying. They rot black overnight. Just
yesterday, they were scarlet like meat under streetlights.
Living is scarier than dying. The wasp trapped under the glass cup
doesn't die.
It stays dying.

I lie motionless like an open gas valve. I dread me. Even as I dread that
no one's here, I dread that someone might be.

Don't you have anything to say?
My mom's words shut the door to my words.

I'm afraid because I have nothing to say.
I'm afraid that I might find something to say.

The things I dread break free. They unburden me like sobbing.
The moment I can't cry, the moment my crying suddenly stops, the
moment the word *scared* loses life, what if I believe! Believe because I
couldn't before?

I'm afraid of the way my drunk friends look at me. I'm afraid of the
way my not-drunk friends look at me.
I'm afraid of the words, *that's why.*

I'm scared of my dad's forefinger. Because only the stump is left. Because there's no fingernail. Because it scratches itchy spots even without a fingernail.

THE LUCKY PAVILION

The curtain of beads clinks together.
A tub of pickled radish sits in the corner.

Whenever I asked my ex
what they wanted to eat, they said, "Black bean noodles." Always black
bean noodles. Watery dregs pooling in the bowls. They mixed rice into
the leftover sauce and shoved a spoon in my face.
"Try a bite."

The black bean noodles come in brass bowls.
I sit on the vinyl floor of The Lucky Pavilion.
Old-fashioned black bean sauce is darker.
It's sweeter.

I used to hate going to the traditional market, the market with that
headless dog lying there, its long tail limp. I hated the fluffy puppy
wagging at its side. I hated the warm clementine wedges that Grandma
peeled and slipped into my hands. My mom stroked my forehead all
night long after scolding me with her hot palm. I dreamed of a dog's
tongue rolling out of her face, gently licking my forehead.

A young Joseonjok woman scrapes off the leftovers with her fingers.
"What a day," she sighs and dumps them into a red tub. She serves me
barley tea with hands smeared in black bean sauce.

Night arrives. Drunk customers retch onto the ground. In the morning, chattering sparrows flock about the vomit like it's a festival. They prance around the bits of rice and squid, pecking cheerfully.

"Good?" "Mhm." I rinse my mouth out with barley tea. A habit from my ex. Love sticks to you like excess. I wish there was a wet tissue to wipe clean my sticky lips and hands.

ETIQUETTE

The family gathers one by one
as if it's a holiday.
They get up again and again

to bring him water
or a blanket.
The more they care for the dog
the more alone it becomes.

The dog gasps.
Like a laugh.
He staggers off the carpet to piss
and collapses.

The whole family surrounds him.
We take turns holding his head.
We watch the young dog die.

"Goodbye, little Kkamji." "Don't tell him to go away. He can
hear you!" "Why don't you go to bed first, Honey. You have work
tomorrow." "I'll wait with you all." "What're we waiting for?"
"I'm going to close his eyes." "Move your hand. He can't breathe."
"He's already dead."

We're silly
as our beloved draws its last breath.

The body is stored in a tomato box
and left in the chill of the front door.
We huddle together and attempt sleep.

THE BOILER ROOM

I wonder about the bone in my hand.
Trash or compost?

Trash is buried
but compost recycled.

Whenever we took out the bones
the dog took off for the boiler room.

Swallowing bones can kill you, but
Dad always chews up his fish bones.

Hey. Eat your food.
The dog sniffed the kibble
and ran off to the boiler room.
In love with bones.

Now there are dog bones in an urn
in the boiler room.
I heard that a company called Angel Pet will make you a necklace
out of your pet's remains.
We discuss this over fried chicken.

I carry the bones
and sneak into the boiler room.

I leave bones
next to the dog's bones
next to the bones of the dog.

TOUCH

The child tries to pick up a baby doll.
A woman scoops up the child.
"Don't touch the hospital's dolls,"
she says. Sick children
were cuddling them.

That's when I remembered
the Yorkshire Terrier we brought home.
Mom put it in the shed
and warned us not to touch him. A newborn
will die from too much handling.

I leave the hospital with my prescription.
In front of the veterinarian's office, in front of the gastroenterologist's
kids are rapping on the show window.
They call out
but the sound is like an infection
to the dogs.

No one touches sick things.
The dead no longer fall sick.
Babies fall gravely ill without warning.
Whenever I fall ill, gravely and without warning
I feel like I'm born again.

I enter the pharmacy and pick up my medicine.
A woman is feeding prescription syrup to her baby.
I go home alone
increasingly afraid of the empty streets.
I look over my shoulder.

No one's there. I'm alone. No one
is touching me.
The thought is comforting.

In the elevator
a child peeks at me.
I'll scare him if I pat his head
so my hand reaches
for my hair.

NEXT, ROCK

There is another me in the next train car. I slide open the door. Me sitting in the car opens the door to the next me.

Mom keeps the window bright until the whole family is home. She stands in the refrigerator light, doors wide open, and snacks on side dishes. The ice in the ice tray ices over. Each one, frosty. The window turns on. Mom strolls around the insides of the ice. I stroll around the terminal's insides, retracing the same path. Am I lost?

Since tomorrow's tomorrow is also tomorrow, I shouldn't worry about tomorrow. I pick up a black rock and toss it onto the black rock beach.

NOT REALLY

I sit by the dog and wait for its owner to show up.

Skateboard across my lap, I watch a bunch of kids skateboard. Three times, the same person walks by. Three times, the dog wags its tail. A kid asks me, "Why are you sitting by yourself? Do you wanna skate with us?" "Not really," I reply. *Not really, not really* . . . I mumble to myself and keep watching the kids. If no one comes, I could just take the dog home. If no one comes, that is.

If only the kids would leave. If only they would talk to me again. The cherry trees liberate petals from their blossoms. Contours of shadows are set free from the shade. Someone's cardigan sits on a bench. Its button dangles off a loose thread, and cherry blossom petals scatter over it like buttons.

The dog rests its head on my feet and falls asleep. I don't know this dog but my feet are bound to it. I watch its nose dry, and I sing it a song. *A long, long time ago, five children disappeared into a far-off corner of the universe. But, oh! They returned as brave warriors. Flashmen! Flashmen! Defenders of Earth!*

I sing low and soft so the dog won't wake, and my quietness makes the plucky theme song melancholic, makes the skateboard heavy, makes the cherry blossoms rush away.

I haven't really, not really, disappeared.

PART 4

PART 4

THE FURTHEST SOUTH

OPEN MOUTH
I open the freezer and look inside my room.

The yellow croaker fish are locked in tight hugs. Face to face with the fish, I dig out my flesh with chopsticks. I pick out the shiny bits of meat and put them in my mouth. The fish mouths also gape wide.

The leftovers look like trash. Still,

WASH HAIR
Someone is standing behind me. Counting my hairs.

My chair pulled out from my desk,
my bare feet sticking out from my blankets
look like a stranger's feet.

To the side, there's an oven, air freshener, handbag, gloves, and textbook. Piled together like that, these things I used to cherish look like a dump.

Power outage. Thunder. A drizzle of rain. A naked baby doll. Its glossy eyes. My grubby toes. My dog's tongue licking the toes. The smell of bread lingers in a paper bag. People light a bonfire on a frozen reservoir. Smoke rises.

My long hairs drip water like a wet drape.
I bend over to wash my hair.
The shower curtain dangles in the air behind me.
Pink mold holds fast to the hems.
Fallen hairs cling to fallen hairs.

Bent at the waist
my hair between my legs
I pump some shampoo and scrub the curtain's hems.

TURN ON THE LIGHTS
I wake up rubbing my nose
and turn on the lights. The pillow is dyed with color.

I lift my head to the ceiling.
Blood flows back into my nose.

Outside my body
the blood spills and nightmares dribble.
Morning throws me out
into the world.

Why? Since when? How come?
The questions travel beyond my body.

I turn off the lights. Blinking, I gaze at the ceiling.

ENDLESSLY

I pluck out a tissue and wipe my lips. The next tissue is already shamelessly poking out of the box. I want to dream about waking from a dream about

waking from a dream. Bad dreams whine at me to play with them. They repeat their game. In the form of a child who died too young.

The bad dreams change faces and reasons. I could say, *There are so many other children like you.*

Or I could not. I listen to the words until the end. I gladly go back to the beginning, even if it looks stupid, like ending cat's cradle in the same position I started in.

Until all of this becomes a memory being abandoned again, abandoned from abandoned memories, abandoned to abandoned memories.

A hollow door opens down the pitch-dark hall. Each hallway fills with light like tissue paper. Like pressing all the buttons in the elevator just for fun. I tear the tissue and

fold a chrysanthemum.
I have to fold and fold and fold the petals.

OPEN FREEZER

Leftover boiled pork in my hand. I open the refrigerator
and find a snowman I made last night.

I put the tiny snowman on my palm.
A cold person should be somewhere cold.

The snowman and I walk
to a slightly colder place
to live longer with my corpses.

South.
An even colder south.

They say penguins don't like the cold.
To survive, they go further
and further, until there are no enemies.

When you become deathly cold
like dead things
I bet pinching flesh brings no pain.
I bet being awake
is like living a dream.

ROOMMATE

1

I, who am not I, dirty the toilet, clean the toilet, steal my soap, use the soap, and share bread with myself.

All night long, I grind my teeth. I wake up from the sound of the grinding, then I get up and sit at the desk to write a letter to my dead self.

When I open the curtains, I see a basketball court and cherry trees, and when I open the curtains, I see cherry trees, and when I open the curtains, I see cherry trees and a pond.

The curtains are like a night sky descended, and the night sky seems like it might open like a curtain, and if the night sky opened eyes would pour out.

I dribble a ball on the basketball court. I throw the ball down, and it soars. It flees from the ground.

By the edge of the pond, I eat the bread. I throw it into the water and make ripples. I do the same with a stone, making ripples. A red mouth emerges from the water, swallowing both bread and stone.

I stand by the window and take a look at myself. Thousands of flower petals fall in the rain. Thousands of waterdrops cling to the window.

2

You, there—with your too-long legs, sitting in the corner of the room again tonight.
I am nearest to the hearth which heats the ondol floor; and you sit in the coldest, farthest spot—
You spread out those long legs like umbrella ribs and wait for something.
With the movements of your slender toe-tips, you spin from thread a room and a hallway.
You show them to me.
A room is forming inside the room.

I think of a young leaf, carefully grooming the fuzz on its back.
I think of Saturn making rings out of dust.
Unwelcome things enter and exit me like a draft.

I become a handle made of iron.
Cold substance approaching a colder substance.
Hold cold things for a long time, and you can meet your own warming temperature.

My friend is cold in my friend's room, and I am cold in mine.

My friend endures that room, and I endure this room.
I rub my feet over my hearth-centered spot on the floor, so I can avoid
going to my friend's room.
Foot thaws foot. Light bulb thaws light bulb.

The hole I noticed outside becomes a window for whoever's inside.
And the small room in the window arrives, as if mailed, to the
opposite window.

You puff your breath out in rings. You move your feet farther away
from the warmth of the hearth.
Innumerable eggs burst out of the clouds of breath like grapes.
The droplets of water on the window sill light up like Christmas.

3
I read a flyer that says: Dog found. Looking for the owner.
It seems the dog's owner has lost her way. She must be intently
wandering around the alleyway fringes.

I'm hesitant to cut across the school grounds, so I
circle around the periphery.
I discover freckles on my arm. New things
keep appearing on my body.

In this neighborhood is the burial mound of a failed emperor. I walk
around the boundary of the mound,

with the people who live there. Grand was the failure of his reign.
The shrine for sacrificial rites is set with
dead people's rice bowls. The rims
shine in the darkness.

A newly opened porridge shop is handing out balloons.
I take one, an outline
filled with air, and I spoon porridge into my mouth.

Next to a sign that says "Need a Date?" are the establishments *Forget-*
Me-Not, and *My Girl,* and *Sunny Day.*
The doors are opened, and the girls have clustered around. *Please don't*
touch or take. Please enjoy with your eyes only.
Potted forget-me-nots are huddled around *Forget-Me-Not.*

4
Should I buy a pet fish tomorrow?
But then the fish's tomorrow would disappear.

I roam around with the bus in the evening.

Completely full of
vacant seats, and between the seats
a jam-packed emptiness.

Back at home
as soon as I turn on the lights, the fluorescent bulbs flicker and die.

The dead bulb in hand, I leave the house.
I find a light bulb that's the same as my light bulb and
I bring it home.

I sit face-to-face with the song playing in the background and eat.

It's a song that I heard yesterday.
And I sing along
with every word.

An empty fish bowl on top of an empty chair.

In the empty fish bowl
soft accompaniment
plays all night long.
And all night long, a gentle wind passes.

The fish
swim out of the mouth
and fly outside.

5
Let's go over there.
I point with my chin at the new cathedral.

To pray?

My friends raise an eyebrow.

The stained glass is so pretty.
If prayer didn't exist, we could all go

together into the cathedral
and talk about how pretty it is.

It's nice that they're not doing mass right now.
While we glance around at the saints, we chatter.

The youth choir is practicing
beautifully singing a serene song.
They almost don't seem human.

The angels are white like snow.
I think if I were to plunge my hand deep inside them
it would be blindingly cold.

The shadow of the stained glass
stretches long over a tall chair.
The sky, Mother Mary, and The Holy Cross
are a rainbow of fragments.

How happy we are because we can't see out the window.
We sit inside the sparkling, multi-colored shadow.

WHAT SONGS DO

Thinking of people
makes us avoid them.
I think we should even avoid we.

Straw spews out when we speak
and becomes a straw doll.

"You left this behind,"
she said. The girl picked up a mirror
that I'd thrown away.
I thanked her
and tried to look glad.

When I come home
I find my room crammed full
of the things I was going to leave on the curb
and the straw we spit up.

I pick off molted cicada skin
just barely hanging onto the ends of the straw.
The song shed us and ran off.
I had to survive.

I crush the emptied body
with my fingers.
Gazing down at the scene,
the song does what songs do.

RED

I heard the word "deer."
Deer run in zigzags as soon as they're born
is what I heard. So they won't get eaten.

I heard the word "girl."
I want to eat
is what I heard.

*

How far can I let my voice spread? What should I do so it doesn't
vanish? My tears turn the whites of my eyes red. If suffering had a
color, I'd be composed of that color. If the window is open, it will
flood out and spread into the gingko tree, then the crosswalk. It'll boil
up and up (open the window please) all the way to a window in the
building across the street. It's the color of suffering, I declare. I trust
that the color of blood is red. My eyes sting. I squint, as if the crimson
sun rises.

There's a line in my journal that goes like this:
Even murderers can't be deprived of their right to pray.
I hesitate between this line and my prayer
that everyone please kill yourselves.

*

I heard if I go there
I won't find a road.

I heard the word "human."
Humans cry the moment they're born
is what I heard.

You're naked, dangled by the ankles
and smacked.
This is the first time
you're required to cry.

Unspeakable suffering is spoken.
An impossible wish comes true.

Congratulations on the suffering.
I set the candle ablaze
with red. I sing.

AUTHOR

Lim Solah is a writer from South Korea. She is the author of the novel The Best Life (Munhakdongnae 2015), the poetry collection Get Packing (Hyeondaemunhak 2020), and the short story collection Snow, Person and Snowperson (Munhakdongnae 2019). She is the recipient of numerous awards such as the JoongAng New Writer's Award for Poetry, Sin Dong-yup Prize for Literature, and the Moonji Literary Award. Lim received the Arts Council Korea's Young Art Frontier Grant in 2014.

TRANSLATORS

Oh Eunkyung and Olan Munson are freelance translators and graduates of the Literature Translation Institute of Korea. Based in Germany, Oh works to introduce contemporary Korean writers to an international readership. Munson is a PhD student in the department of Comparative Literature at the University of Michigan. In 2017, they won the Korea Times Modern Korean Literature Translation Commendation Award in fiction for their co-translation of Choi Eunyoung's short story "Xin chào, Xin chào."

ABOUT THE SERIES

The Moon Country Korean Poetry Series publishes new English translations of contemporary Korean poetry by both mid-career and up-and-coming poets who debuted after the IMF crisis. By introducing work which comes out of our shared milieu, this series not only aims to widen the field of contemporary Korean poetry available in English translation, but also to challenge orientalist, neo-colonial, and national literature discourses. Our hope is that readers will inhabit these books as bodies of experience rather than view them as objects of knowledge, that they will allow themselves to be altered by them, and emerge from the page with eyes that seem to see "a world that belongs to another star."